remember

the alamo

Texians, Tejanos, and Mexicans Tell Their Stories

PAUL ROBERT WALKER

NATIONAL GEOGRAPHIC

WASHINGTON, D.C.

For the brave on both sides, with hope for better understanding between our nations.

John M. Fahey, Jr., *President and Chief Executive Officer*
Gilbert M. Grosvenor, *Chairman of the Board*
Nina D. Hoffman, *Executive Vice President,*
 President Book Publishing Group

STAFF FOR THIS BOOK
Nancy Laties Feresten, *Vice President, Editor-in-Chief*
 of Children's Books
Suzanne Patrick Fonda, *Project Editor*
David M. Seager, *Art Director*
Lori Epstein, *Illustrations Editor*
Carl Mehler, *Director of Maps*
Justin Morrill, The M Factory, Inc., *Map Research and*
 Production
Rebecca Baines, *Editorial Assistant*
Ruthie Thompson, *Production Designer*
Elisabeth MacRae Bobynskyj, *Indexer*
Debbie Guthrie Haer, *Copy Editor*
R. Gary Colbert, *Production Director*
Lewis R. Bassford, *Production Manager*
Nicole Elliott, Vincent P. Ryan, and Maryclare Tracey,
 Manufacturing Managers

Text is set in ITC New Baskerville.

ACKNOWLEDGMENTS
First and foremost, thanks to Bruce Winders at the Alamo and Martha
Utterback at the Daughters of the Republic of Texas Library for their
unwavering support above and beyond the call of duty. Bruce and
Martha live and breathe this story every day, and they and their staffs
have been helpful in too many ways to list here. Many others have
helped me along the way, including (but not limited to) Stephen
Harrigan, Alan C. Huffines, Thomas Ricks Lindley, Timothy M. Matovina,
and Gary S. Zaboly. The staff at all of the organizations listed in the
photo credits at right were also outstanding, and I wish that I could
thank them personally. Finally, a big thanks to my long-time friend, Luz
Maria Prieto-Wilmot, for welcoming me into her San Antonio home.

One of the world's largest nonprofit scientific and educational
organizations, the National Geographic Society was founded in 1888
"for the increase and diffusion of geographic knowledge." Fulfilling this
mission, the Society educates and inspires millions every day through
its magazines, books, television programs, videos, maps and atlases,
research grants, the National Geographic Bee, teacher workshops, and
innovative classroom materials. The Society is supported through
membership dues, charitable gifts, and income from the sale of its
educational products. This support is vital to National Geographic's
mission to increase global understanding and promote conservation
of our planet through exploration, research, and education. For more
information, please call 1-800-NGS LINE (647-5463) or write to the
following address:

NATIONAL GEOGRAPHIC SOCIETY
1145 17th Street N.W.
Washington, D.C. 20036-4688 U.S.A.

Visit the Society's Web site: www.nationalgeographic.com

Printed in China

Library of Congress Cataloging-in Publication Data
Walker, Paul Robert.
 Remember the Alamo : Texians, Tejanos, and Mexicans tell their
stories / by Paul Robert Walker.
  p. cm.
 Includes bibliographical references and index.
  ISBN-13: 978-1-4263-0010-3 (hardcover)
  ISBN-13: 978-1-4263-0011-0 (library)
1. Alamo (San Antonio, Tex.)—Siege, 1836. 2. Texas—History—
Revolution, 1835–1836—Personal narratives—Juvenile literature.
I. National Geographic Society (U.S.) II. Title.
 F390.W175 2007
 976.4'03—dc22
                        2006034497

For information about special discounts for bulk purchases,
please contact National Geographic Books Special Sales:
ngspecsales@ngs.org.

The front of the Alamo church as it appears today.
The distinctive bell-shaped structure at the top was added
during a rebuilding project between 1850 and 1852, ordered by the U.S. Army,
in which a roof was also added and other major repairs were made.

Few battles in American history are as celebrated as the Battle of the Alamo. For 13 days in 1836, a small band of rebels defending an old Spanish mission called the Alamo held out against overwhelming odds. Outside the walls was the Mexican Army commanded in person by Mexico's president—General Antonio López de Santa Anna. Most of the men trapped inside the Alamo had come from the United States, either as colonists before the revolution or as volunteers who came to help after the war started. Inside, too, were a number of *Tejanos,* or Mexican Texans, who were as committed as the Texians to being free of a ruler who had no regard for democratic values.

The siege came to a bloody end on the morning of March 6, 1836, when Santa Anna's soldiers attacked and killed the entire Alamo garrison. The valiant effort of the defenders, though, earned them a special place in history. "Remember the Alamo!" became the rallying cry that drove the Texians and their Tejano allies on to ultimately win their independence from Mexico.

The story of the Alamo quickly became enshrined by early historians. Novelists and filmmakers also have found an eager audience for a tale that pitted freedom-loving Texians against the dictatorial Santa Anna, starring the larger-than-life American folk heroes David Crockett and James Bowie as well as Texas legends Stephen F. Austin, Sam Houston, and William B. Travis. Fact and fiction blended to create a good story.

A good story, though, isn't always good history. Paul Robert Walker provides readers with a fresh perspective on the Battle of the Alamo by giving them more than just well-worn legends and myths. Guided by historians who have looked beyond the popular images of the Alamo, Walker discovered that the Texas Revolution—the setting for the Alamo—is a very complex chapter in American history. To appreciate it fully, readers need to understand who the rebels were and why they were attempting to break away from Mexico.

Walker provides the answers by introducing readers to Mexicans, Texians, and Tejanos and the issues they faced in the world of 1836. They will discover that what is now Texas, as well as the land west of it, was part of the Republic of Mexico; that the desire for cheap land made some Americans become Mexican citizens; that many Mexicans were as angry as the American immigrants that liberties promised in Mexico's Constitution of 1824 were being trampled by the government; and that the clash between these opposing forces would lead to revolution.

Although the Texas Revolution has long passed, the events of 1836 are still important. They are part of the shared history that connects the United States and Mexico. The story of the Alamo provides a perfect gateway to learning about the development of the two nations. Understanding what happened in the past can help shed light on current issues and pave the way for better relations between our two countries in the present.

Richard Bruce Winders, Ph.D.
Alamo Curator and Historian

A scout brings word of an Indian attack, and Stephen F. Austin grabs his rifle
to defend his colony in this painting by Henry A. McArdle. Austin's cook,
Simon, is at the window, while a Mexican land agent (left) and surveyor sit
on the floor. The secretary of the colony and the chief scout look on.

call to arms

On the morning of June 29, 1835, 25 armed men boarded a sloop—a wooden ship with one mast and two sails—at Lynch's Ferry, on the San Jacinto River near the present site of Houston, Texas. A small cannon, mounted on wooden wheels, had already been loaded onto the deck. The men were on a mission that many fellow citizens considered foolish and that the Republic of Mexico—their government—considered treason.

All of the men were Americans, but they were living in Texas, which at that time was part of Mexico. Some had entered Texas legally under a program established by the Mexican government to draw more settlers to the remote frontier. Others were illegal immigrants, looking for any opportunity they could grab. Legal or illegal, they called themselves Texians.

Their leader was a 25-year-old lawyer and newspaper publisher named William Barret Travis. He had come to Texas four years earlier and legally obtained land from Stephen F. Austin, the first and greatest of the *empresarios*—men who signed agreements with the Mexican government to bring settlers to Texas. More people were needed to help defend the sparsely populated region against Indian attack, so the government of Mexico opened its doors to immigrants from the United States and Europe. It got more than it bargained for.

In 1834, a year before Travis set out from Lynch's Ferry, a Mexican colonel named Juan Almonte toured Texas and counted the population. He estimated that there were almost 4,000 Mexican Texans *(Tejanos),* some 15,000 Americans (Texians)—including Europeans who had passed through America—and another 600 immigrants in an Irish colony. The Americans owned about 2,000 black slaves, who worked on farms and cotton plantations. This caused constant conflict with Mexican authorities because slavery was illegal in Mexico. Almonte wrote, ". . . if we do not stop the flow [of slaves] quickly, it will be difficult to correct it later without causing a revolution of far-reaching consequences."

William Barret Travis

Colonel Juan Almonte

Colonel Almonte was right that a revolution was coming to Texas, and Travis and his men were trying to start it on that June morning in 1835. However, the issue that day was not slavery; it was the customs house at Fort Anahuac, on the Texas coast. A small group of soldiers there tried to enforce Mexican law by collecting taxes on goods imported into Mexico. On June 12, a fight had broken out between the soldiers and three Texians suspected of smuggling. One Texian was wounded and all three were imprisoned, though two were quickly released.

News of this incident reached San Felipe de Austin—where Travis had his law office—about a week later. Then, on June 21, the citizens of San Felipe intercepted a messenger carrying a letter to the commander at Anahuac, indicating that more Mexican troops would soon arrive in Texas to enforce Mexican law. By this time, the Texians had heard other disturbing news from south of the Rio Grande.

A civil war was raging in Mexico, sparked by the Mexican president, General Antonio López de Santa Anna, who was working to overthrow the Constitution of 1824—modeled after the U.S. Constitution—and establish himself as a military dictator. That spring, Santa Anna had personally led his army to put down a rebellion in the state of Zacatecas. After defeating the rebel forces, he allowed his soldiers to raid the capital, stealing what they wanted, killing hundreds if not thousands of men, and abusing the women. Another army, under General Martín Perfecto de Cos, had invaded Coahuila, broken up the state congress, and imprisoned the governor. At this time, Texas was joined with Coahuila in a single state, called *Coahuila y Tejas* in Spanish. Neither the Texians nor the Tejanos liked this arrangement, but an attack on the government in Coahuila was a serious threat to Texas.

In this atmosphere of growing tension, the Texians in San Felipe and the surrounding area held a public meeting on June 22. The chairman of the meeting was a fellow lawyer and friend of Travis named Robert M. Williamson—nicknamed "Three-Legged Willie" because he had a wooden leg and walked with a cane. Williamson later published a clear and passionate explanation of why this meeting was called:

Robert M. Williamson

"Your republican form of Government is broken down[,] your state authorities have by the military been driven from the exercise of their constitutional duties, and detain in custody the Governor of your State, and of your choice. Not only in Coahuila and Texas—has this arbitrary and despotic course been pursued, but other states of the [Mexican] federation mourn the loss of their constitutions and their liberties and at this moment the proud and gallant & republic[an] State of Zacatecas mourns the loss of two thousand citizens, slain in battle by the troops of Gen. Santa Anna, and the survivors now endure the galling chains of military rule.—Durango and other states have also fallen beneath the rule of military power, and every state and province of the Mexican Republic (excepting Texas) have submitted to the Dictator."

Despite the strong feelings of men like Williamson and Travis, no plan of action was adopted at the meeting. A majority of Texians and Tejanos still believed that there might be a peaceful solution to the civil war, and they hoped to avoid bloodshed in Texas. Travis and a small group of other men held a second meeting that very night and vowed to disarm the Mexican force at Anahuac.

A week later, these Texians sailed down the San Jacinto River into Trinity Bay, turning north toward Anahuac. Around three or four that afternoon, their boat ran aground a half mile offshore from the town. After a booming shot to announce their presence, the cannon was lowered into a small boat that came out to meet them. The men got into this and another boat and rowed to shore.

In 1832, William Travis and his law partner, Patrick Jack, were imprisoned for defying Mexican authorities at Fort Anahuac (above). A small army of Texians forced their release and drove the soldiers out of Texas. In 1835, the soldiers returned, and Travis got his revenge.

Onshore, Travis exchanged notes with the Mexican commander, Captain Antonio Tenorio, demanding that Tenorio and his soldiers surrender immediately. Just after sunset, the Texians headed for the fort, pulling their little cannon and lighting their way with blazing torches. They found the fort deserted. Tenorio and his men—about 40 in all—had retreated to a grove of trees on the bank of the Trinity River, some 200 yards away.

Travis ordered a blast from his cannon, which prompted another note from Captain Tenorio, asking for a meeting. In the moonlight, with armed men on both sides covering the two officers, Travis threatened to "put every man to the sword" if they did not surrender within 15 minutes. It was a bold threat, but Tenorio had no artillery to match the Texians' cannon, and he did not know how many men were hidden among the trees. Tenorio consulted his officers, and they decided "in view of the difficulty and uselessness of making a defense, that a capitulation [surrender] should be made."

Travis and his captives arrived at the small town of Harrisburg, near Lynch's Ferry, on the 4th of July, just in time for a big Texas barbeque. Many years later, an American woman named Dilue Rose Harris—just ten years old at the time—remembered that "Captain Tenorio walked among the people shaking hands with the men and acting as if he was the hero of the occasion."

The next day, on the 5th, the Texians held a dance. "The Mexican officers were at the ball," Harris recalled. "They did not dance country dances." Most Mexican officers were more educated than Americans on the frontier, so they danced European-style dances, and many spoke French as well as Spanish. A German woman at the ball also spoke French, and she and Captain Tenorio "danced and talked [in French] all the evening. She was handsome and he a fine looking man, and they attracted a great deal of attention."

While the Mexican officers enjoyed Texas hospitality, Travis was considered a dangerous troublemaker by many fellow Texians. "The disarming of the

Dilue Rose Harris

garrison at Anahuac was not approved by the older citizens," Harris wrote. "Those who had families with all they possessed in Texas wished rather to pay duties to Mexico than to fight." Travis had a family, too, but he had left them behind in Alabama to create a new life in Texas.

The attack on Anahuac divided the Texians into two political parties: the Peace Party, those who still believed that Texas might find a peaceful solution to the conflict with Santa Anna's government, and the War Party or "Wardogs," men like Travis and Williamson, who believed the only solution was war. Beyond this local conflict was the violent and bitter conflict raging throughout Mexico, which now threatened to spread into Texas.

Mexico had been independent from Spain for 14 years, and throughout that time there had been near-constant violence over how the new country should be governed. Santa Anna and his supporters were called Centralists, because they believed in a strong central government, a strong Catholic Church, a strong army, and the protection of wealthy landowners. Opposing them were the Federalists, who believed in more freedom for the states, less power for the Church and army, and a fairer distribution of land. Almost all Texas citizens—Texians and Tejanos, Peace Party and Wardogs—were Federalists, who believed in the democratic freedoms promised by the Mexican Constitution of 1824.

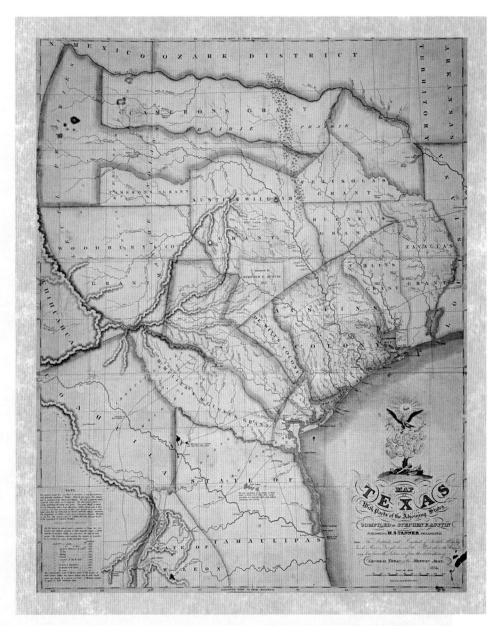

This 1835 edition of Stephen Austin's 1830 map shows that Mexico had granted most of the land in Texas to land agents called empresarios. Some empresarios were American; others were Mexican or European. The largest Mexican population was in and around San Antonio de Béxar (Bexar on the map), which was not part of a land grant.

For the month of July, the Peace Party dominated Texas politics. Travis was so stung by criticism of his actions at Anahuac that he promised to publish an explanation. Before he did so, General Cos ordered the regional political chief—a Texian Peace Party leader—to immediately arrest "the ungrateful and bad citizen, W. B. Travis who headed the revolutionary party. . .in order that he may be tried and punished according to Law." Cos also ordered the arrest of other rebel leaders, including Mexican Federalist statesman Lorenzo de Zavala, who had taken refuge in Texas after resigning his position as minister to France in protest over Santa Anna's policies. By this time, additional Mexican troops had arrived in Texas with reports of more on the way.

The arrest orders changed the attitude of the Peace Party. They did not like what Travis had done, but they were not going to turn him or other rebels over to Mexican "Law"—not when Santa Anna ignored the greatest law of all, the Constitution of 1824.

They also knew that a man could disappear in the Mexican legal system. Stephen F. Austin, the greatest empresario and the man most admired by the Peace Party, had gone to Mexico City in 1833 to present a series of requests to the recently elected president, General Santa Anna. Although usually a moderate man who believed in working with Mexican authorities, Austin became frustrated while waiting to meet with Santa Anna and wrote a letter from Mexico City suggesting, "The fate of Texas depends upon itself and not upon this government;. . .[Texas] is lost if its inhabitants do not take its affairs into their own hands."

This letter was as rash and treasonous as the attack on Anahuac, and—after the letter fell into government hands—Austin was arrested and imprisoned for more than a year. Even after his release, he was not allowed to leave the capital. Texians of both political parties agreed that Austin's long imprisonment was unjust, and they would not expose Travis to the same threat.

The cathedral of Mexico City, shown in this painting from the mid-1830s, symbolizes the power of the Catholic Church in Mexico. The capital city, almost 1,000 miles from the Texas settlements, was an elegant contrast to the rough Texas frontier.

General Martín Perfecto de Cos

Stephen F. Austin

On September 1, 1835, Travis finally wrote his explanation for the Anahuac attack: "I volunteered in that expedition, with no other motives than of patriotism and a wish to aid my suffering countrymen in the embarrassing strait to which they were likely to be reduced by military tyranny. . . .Time alone will show whether the step was correct or not. And time will show that when this country [Texas] is in danger that I will show myself as patriotic and ready to serve her as those who to save themselves have disavowed the act and denounced me to the usurping military."

The same day that Travis wrote his explanation, Austin returned to Texas. He had been gone a total of 28 months. Austin was sick and weak from his long imprisonment, but he was a man who could unite the Texians in their response to the Mexican government.

In mid-September, General Cos landed with 400 troops at Copano Bay on the Texas coast. He demanded that the Texians surrender their weapons and their radical leaders immediately, or he would invade the American settlements. This was the moment of truth, and Stephen F. Austin—who had always been a man of peace—now threw his voice behind the War Party. "WAR is our only resource," he announced, "—there is no other remedy but to defend our rights, our country and ourselves by force of arms."

The Texas Revolution was about to begin, and the battle road would lead through an old Spanish mission called the Alamo.

The men of Gonzales defiantly display their "Come and Take It" flag as they defend their little cannon in this mural at the Gonzales Memorial Museum. A small cannon on display at the museum may or may not be the original Gonzales cannon. As with many Texas legends, the truth may never be known.

CHAPTER 2 ——————

come and take it!

Although all of Texas belonged to Mexico, there were really two different Texases by 1835. The rolling grasslands and coastal plains of eastern Texas were dominated by American settlements. There were substantial Tejano settlements at Nacogdoches, near the Louisiana border, and at Goliad and Victoria, near the Gulf of Mexico. The largest Tejano population, however, and the heart of Mexican Texas was farther west in and around San Antonio de Béxar—often called simply Béxar or Béjar—nestled into a bend of the San Antonio River.

Across the river from San Antonio was the old Spanish mission of San Antonio de Valero, the first of five missions in the area, built to convert the local Indians to Christianity and to teach them skills to live as Spanish citizens. In 1793, after the Indians were considered "civilized," the mission was given to the Mexican Army. It was never a true fort, but it housed soldiers and offered protection against Indian attacks. In 1803, a group of soldiers arrived from the small town of San José y Santiago del Alamo in Coahuila, and the old mission became known as the Alamo, the Spanish word for a cottonwood tree.

By September 1835, there were more than 400 Mexican soldiers at the Alamo, with many new arrivals sent to reinforce the post in preparation for possible military action against the Texians. Captain Tenorio and his men—who had been released by Travis on the promise not to fight against Texas—also arrived at the Alamo that month, after a long delay in San Felipe de Austin.

On September 20, in response to General Cos's order to disarm the Texians, the Alamo commander, Colonel Domingo de Ugartechea, sent a corporal with several soldiers to the American settlement of Gonzales to take back a small cannon the settlers had been given to protect themselves against Indian attack. Gonzales was the closest American settlement to San Antonio, about 70 miles to the east, and the settlers were usually moderate in their views. But they decided that this cannon was worth fighting for.

When the people of Gonzales refused to give up the cannon, Colonel Ugartechea sent a larger force of 100 cavalrymen under Lieutenant Francisco Castañeda. Knowing the soldiers would come, the settlers moved their women and children to safety and buried the cannon in a peach orchard. They assembled the only fighting men they had—18 colonists still called "The Old Eighteen" in Gonzales today—and sent out messages to other American settlements, asking for reinforcements.

On September 29, the soldiers reached the Guadalupe River, swollen from recent rains. The colonists had hidden the boat used as a ferry at the crossing, and the Old Eighteen waited with their guns on the other side. For two days, the colonists stalled, telling Lieutenant Castañeda that the *alcalde,* or mayor, Andrew Ponton, was away and there could be no decision until he returned.

By the evening of September 30, there were about 150 armed Texians in Gonzales. Several men dug up the little cannon and mounted it on wooden wheels, just as Travis's men had mounted their cannon three months earlier. They cut up pieces of scrap metal for ammunition, and two women made a battle flag out of a wedding dress. It had a big black image of the cannon in the middle, with a lone star above it. Below were fighting words: "Come and Take It."

On the night of October 1, the Texians crossed the Guadalupe River and marched toward the Mexican position. Charles Mason later recalled, "The whole force were mustered to listen to a patriotic address, and a fervent appeal to the God of battles, in its behalf and for its success, by the Rev. Doctor Smith, as chaplain. The little army, full of hope and high in spirit, took up the line of march, through a dense fog, for the enemy's camp; calculating to surprise him, but was prevented by the continued barking of a dog that had followed, causing the vanguard to be fired upon by the enemy's picket-guard." Amid the Mexican fire, one Texian fell from his horse and suffered a bloody nose.

At dawn on October 2, the Texians found themselves in a wooded area along the river, with a cornfield and watermelon patch between them and the Mexican soldiers. The fog was still thick, but the men advanced, firing their long-range rifles at whatever they could see. Castañeda ordered a charge by 40 cavalrymen.

Alcalde *Andrew Ponton*

The Texians retreated to the woods but stopped the charge with a rifle volley and a blast of scrap metal from their little cannon. Later, when the fog lifted, Castañeda asked for a meeting. He wanted to know why he was being attacked.

John H. Moore, who had been elected colonel by the colonists, invited the lieutenant and his men to join the Texians as Mexican Federalists fighting for the Constitution of 1824 against the illegal Centralist government of Santa Anna. Castañeda replied that he was a Federalist, too, and so were most of his men, but they were soldiers who had to obey orders. The officers went back to their armies, and Moore led his men forward, shouting, "Charge 'em, boys, and give 'em hell." The little cannon blasted again, and Castañeda ordered a full retreat, leaving most of their supplies behind. One Mexican soldier was wounded.

As news of the battle spread through Texas, men poured into Gonzales. In the meantime, a group of more than 100 Texians and Tejanos attacked the old Spanish presidio at Goliad, about 60 miles south of Gonzales. Unlike the Alamo, the presidio was a true fort, built to protect the road from the Gulf of Mexico to San Antonio. General Cos had recently passed through on his way to San Antonio, but he had not left reinforcements, so there were only about 50 men to defend the fort.

Late on the night of October 9, the rebels smashed through the wooden door of the commander's quarters with axes supplied by local Tejanos. After a brief skirmish, the Texian interpreter shouted, "They say they will massacre everyone of you, unless you come out immediately and surrender. Come out—come out quick. I cannot keep them back." The Mexicans surrendered immediately.

On the morning of October 2, 1835, the defenders of Gonzales dare the Mexican soldiers under Lieutenant Castañeda to "come and take" their little cannon. This drawing by Charles Shaw is more accurate in the depictions of clothing and weapons than the mural on page 18.

Colonel John H. Moore

Texian volunteer

With the capture of Goliad, the Texians cut off the supply route from the sea for General Cos. He was now in San Antonio with his troops and could only be supplied from Mexico City by the long overland road through the deserts of northern Mexico.

Two days later, on October 11, Austin arrived in Gonzales. By this time there were about 300 fighting men there, organized into companies with elected officers. This was the democratic way that militias had always organized on the American frontier. But now these volunteer companies had become a small army, and they needed a leader. That day, the officers unanimously elected Stephen F. Austin—still sick and exhausted from his long imprisonment—"commander-in-chief of the volunteer army of Texas."

The volunteers at Gonzales brought their own weapons and wore whatever clothes they had. Many carried long Kentucky hunting rifles, which were deadly from a distance. Others had shotguns or pistols, while some had no weapons at all—which didn't matter, because there was not enough gunpowder and ammunition. Most men wore buckskin breeches and moccasins or shoes instead of boots. Some wore military-style caps, but many wore sombreros, top hats, and coonskin caps.

A blacksmith named Noah Smithwick, who joined the Texas army the day after the Gonzales battle, later recalled that it was "a fantastic military array to a casual observer, but the one great purpose animating every heart clothed us in a uniform more perfect to our eyes than was ever donned by regulars on dress parade." Actually the purpose was almost as varied as the uniforms, as Smithwick admitted: "I can not remember that there was any distinct understanding as to the position we were to assume toward Mexico. Some were for independence; some for the Constitution of 1824; and some for anything, just so it was a row. But we were all ready to fight."

With Austin in command, the ragtag army moved toward San Antonio, picking up men along the way. One of them was James Bowie, already famous as a fighter on the American and Mexican frontiers. Austin appointed Bowie a colonel. Among other officers appointed by Austin were Lieutenant William B.

Noah Smithwick

Samuel McCulloch, Jr., a "Free Negro" who had come to Texas in 1835 with his family, was badly wounded during the attack on the Goliad presidio and was later described as "the first [Texian] whose blood was shed in the War of Independence." Although the Texas Constitution denied citizenship to African Americans, McCulloch received special treatment and a land grant. He married a white woman—despite a law against such marriages—raised a family, and fought for Texas in later battles.

Travis, who was ordered to form a company of cavalry; Captain James Fannin, who had attended West Point for two years; and Captain Ben Milam, who commanded a spy company. Milam, who had first come to Texas in 1818, had served as a colonel in the Mexican Army and was addressed as "Colonel" out of respect.

Local Tejano leaders also joined Austin's army, including the former alcalde of San Antonio Juan Seguín, who rode into camp and informed Austin that many people in San Antonio supported the rebellion. That spring, Seguín had led a group of men into Coahuila to help the Federalist governor fight against General Cos. When that effort failed, Seguín recalled, "We pledged ourselves to use all our influence to rouse Texas against the tyrannical government of Santa Anna."

Austin appointed Seguín a captain and asked him to return with a company of Tejano horsemen. Another Mexican alcalde, Plácido Benavides—who had fought with the Texians at Goliad—arrived with some 30 Tejano riders. The Tejanos knew the countryside and served as guides, scouts, and messengers.

By late October, Austin had around 600 men under his command. The Texian army approached San Antonio from the south, moving up the chain

Captain Juan Seguín

of missions along the San Antonio River. On October 27, Austin sent 92 men under Bowie and Fannin to look for a new position closer to the city. Led by Bowie's friend Juan Seguín, they reached Mission Concepción and camped for the night near a bend in the river. The next morning, in a dense fog, they were awakened by musket fire from an enemy they could not see. "When the fog rose," Bowie wrote, "it was apparent to all that we were surrounded, and a desperate fight was inevitable, all communications with the main army being cut off."

The 92 men faced a Mexican force of some 300 cavalry and 100 infantry. According to Bowie, "The discharge from the enemy was one continued blaze of fire, whilst that from our lines, was more slowly delivered, but with good aim and deadly effect." The "deadly effect" of the Texians' Kentucky rifles could kill a man from 200 yards away, while the muskets of the Mexican soldiers were only effective from about 70 yards.

Colonel James Bowie

This long hunting rifle belonged to David Crockett, the most famous of the Alamo defenders. The "Bowie knife" below it was designed by James Bowie's brother Reza. Bowie and other Alamo defenders carried similar knives.

When the Mexicans began firing a cannon, the Texians shot the artillerymen. "Three times we picked off their gunners," recalled Noah Smithwick, "the last one with a lighted match in his hand." Shouting "the cannon and victory," the Texians moved toward the cannon and the soldiers retreated, leaving the cannon behind. Bowie claimed that 76 Mexican soldiers were killed or wounded, while the Texians only lost a single man.

Austin and the rest of the Texas army arrived a half hour later, and the full army now moved on to San Antonio. General Cos's men had built up the fortifications at the Alamo and in San Antonio, turning it into a fort-city. The forces were fairly equal, but Cos had about 20 cannons, the largest collection of artillery west of the Mississippi. Austin knew it would be suicide to launch an immediate attack, but he also knew that it would be difficult to wait too long with

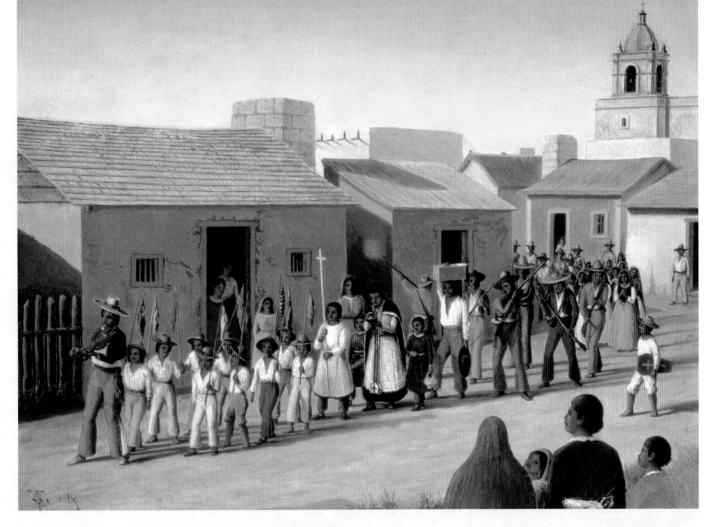

a volunteer army. Two hundred men left in the first few days, but others arrived to take their places, drawn from the United States by the promise of adventure and free land, offered by the Texians to anyone who would join their revolution.

For the month of November, Austin's army camped outside San Antonio while other Texian leaders held a convention, called the Consultation, in San Felipe de Austin. There the Peace Party and War Party argued over the purpose of the rebellion. The Peace Party believed they were fighting as Mexican Federalists to restore Mexico's Constitution of 1824, while the War Party saw the rebellion as a war for independence, similar to the American Revolution. The two sides reached a compromise, and on November 7 issued a public statement called the Declaration of Causes.

On the one hand, they declared, the people of Texas had "taken up arms in defence of their *rights* and *liberties,* which are threatened by the encroachments of *military despots,* and in defence of the republican principles of the Federal Constitution of Mexico, of 1824." On the other hand, they claimed the right "during the disorganization of the Federal System, and the reign of despotism,

While eastern Texas was home to Protestant Americans living on Mexican soil, San Antonio was a Catholic Mexican city much like other cities in Mexico. This painting by French-born San Antonio artist Theodore Gentilz captures a colorful funeral procession for an infant, who— according to Catholic belief—would join the angels in heaven.

to withdraw from the Union [of Mexico], to establish an independent government, or to adopt such measures as they may deem best calculated to protect their rights and liberties."

The Consultation established a government to rule Texas during the rebellion. A War Party leader named Henry Smith was elected governor and a General Council was formed to help him govern. The roles of the governor and council were not clear, and this would cause serious problems.

The Consultation also established the basic structure for a regular army and appointed Sam Houston as commander-in-chief. Houston was a hero from the War of 1812, a former governor of Tennessee, and a trusted friend of President Andrew Jackson. In time, he would prove a great commander, but in November 1835, he commanded an army that did not exist, since all the men fighting were volunteers under their elected commander Stephen F. Austin.

In late November, Austin left the volunteer army. On assignment from the General Council in San Felipe, he and two other men left for Washington, D.C.,

According to fellow officer Frank Johnson, Ben Milam (waving his hat)—after receiving permission from General Burleson to ask for volunteers—called in a clear, loud voice, "Who will go with Old Ben Milam into San Antonio?" Many men shouted, "I will!" and Milam told them to get in line. About 300 men volunteered.

and other cities to ask for help from the United States. This was an important mission, but it took Austin out of Texas for the rest of the war.

Edward Burleson, a veteran of the War of 1812 and an experienced Indian fighter, was elected commander of the volunteers and made plans to attack San Antonio on December 4. However, a majority of his officers voted against the attack, so Burleson ordered a retreat to Gonzales.

General Edward Burleson

Colonel Ben Milam, who had been out scouting, rode into camp on December 4 to discover the men preparing to withdraw. After a heated discussion, Burleson agreed that Milam could ask for volunteers to attack San Antonio. If enough men were willing to attack, Burleson would hold the others "in reserve" to protect the base camp and cover a retreat if necessary.

Early the next morning, Milam attacked with about 300 men. James Neill, an experienced artilleryman, led a small group that fired a cannon at the Alamo to keep the Mexican soldiers pinned down while two columns of Texians and Tejanos stormed into the city. One was led by Milam, the other by Colonel Frank Johnson. They moved from house to house, street to street, and plaza to plaza, smashing through adobe walls and lowering themselves through rooftops, while dodging Mexican sharpshooters and a steady pounding of cannonballs.

Ben Milam was killed on December 7 with a single rifle shot to the head, but the others kept fighting. By the following morning, the Texians controlled San Antonio with minimal casualties, while General Cos, who had retreated into the Alamo, had lost some 150 men in the fighting and perhaps 150 more to desertion.

Colonel Frank Johnson

On December 9, Cos raised a white flag of surrender over the Alamo. In an agreement signed two days later, he pledged that he and his men would leave Texas and never fight again against the Constitution of 1824. "All has been lost save honor," wrote one Mexican officer. "We were surrounded with crude bumpkins, proud and overbearing."

Those crude bumpkins now controlled the Alamo.

Micajah Autry, portrayed defending the Alamo, was a teacher and lawyer who left his family in Tennessee to seek a better life for them in Texas. "I go the whole Hog in the cause of Texas," he wrote to his wife. "I expect to help them gain their independence . . . for it is worth risking many lives for."

defending the Alamo

On December 5, the day the battle for San Antonio began, General Santa Anna arrived in San Luis Potosí, some 700 miles to the south, to assemble an army and regain control of his rebellious frontier. Two days later, he issued an order that would define the coming battles: "The foreigners who are making war against the Mexican nation, violating all laws, are not deserving of any consideration, and for that reason no quarter will be given them. . . .They have, with audacity, declared a war of extermination to the Mexicans, and they should be treated the same way."

In military language, "no quarter" means no mercy, no paroles, no prisoners. As Santa Anna would learn, the Texians and Tejanos had not declared "a war of extermination" and did parole General Cos and his soldiers. No such mercy would be shown the Texas rebels.

Santa Anna used his own money and borrowed money from anyone who would lend it to assemble and equip an army of more than 6,000 soldiers. By late December, they were marching northward toward Texas. They suffered greatly crossing the deserts of northern Mexico in freezing cold and blinding blizzards. Yet they marched on, driven by the steel will of General Santa Anna.

Texas leaders knew an army would come, but they believed that mid-April was the earliest it could arrive, and they did not know where it would attack. Sam Houston made plans to defend three key places: the Alamo, the presidio at Goliad, and the beach at Copano, where Houston hoped to bring in supplies and reinforcements from the United States. This was a logical plan, but Texas leaders became distracted by another plan to attack the city of Matamoros, in the Mexican state of Tamaulipas. It was a wild and dangerous idea that split the Texas government and army at the time that Texas faced its greatest danger.

Although Governor Smith and General Houston approved the Matamoros expedition at first, they quickly saw that it was a bad military idea, because it

General Santa Anna

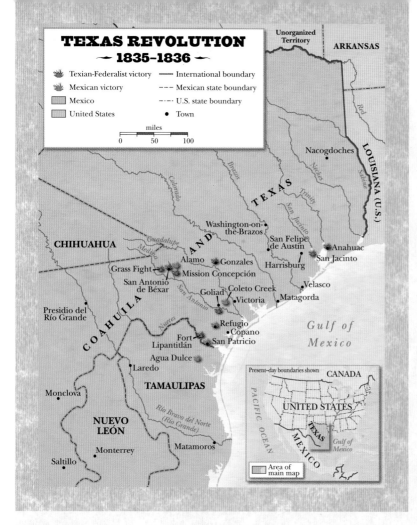

TEXAS REVOLUTION
~ 1835–1836 ~

- Texian-Federalist victory
- Mexican victory
- Mexico
- United States
- —— International boundary
- --- Mexican state boundary
- ·-·- U.S. state boundary
- • Town

miles
0   50   100

The Texas Revolution took place in two phases. In 1835, the Texian-Federalist forces won every battle, beginning with Anahuac and Gonzales and ending with the surrender of General Cos in San Antonio. The storming of the Alamo in 1836 was the first in a series of victories for Mexico. Yet, after a string of defeats, the Texians triumphed at San Jacinto. It was the one victory they needed to win independence.

would spread the small Texas army too thin. They also believed it was a diplomatic mistake. Both Smith and Houston strongly favored independence for Texas. Attacking Matamoros had nothing to do with independence. How could they expect support from the United States and other countries if they invaded another Mexican state?

Some members of the General Council still saw the revolution as a fight for the Mexican Constitution of 1824. By attacking Matamoros, they hoped to inspire other Mexican Federalists to join them. For most council members, however, and for the officers and volunteers who agreed to launch the attack, the real appeal was money. Matamoros was a busy port. If they captured it, they could collect taxes to support their revolution and help themselves to whatever Mexican wealth they might plunder.

In early January 1836, the council appointed two different men to raise an army and lead the Matamoros expedition: Colonel Frank Johnson, who had led the volunteers into San Antonio with Ben Milam, and James Fannin, who was now a colonel in the regular Texas army. Sharing leadership with Johnson was a Scottish doctor named James Grant, who had vast land holdings in Coahuila that he wanted to protect.

At this time, Johnson was commander of the volunteers at the Alamo, because Edward Burleson had gone home for the winter. Many others had also left, and Johnson and Grant took about 200 of those who remained—two-thirds of the total force. Just as important, they took clothing, food, medicine, supplies, horses, and mules that the Alamo defenders needed to get through the winter.

With the departure of Colonel Johnson, command of the Alamo went to Lieutenant Colonel James Neill, whose knowledge of artillery had played a key role in the victories at Gonzales and San Antonio. After taking command, Neill sent a desperate letter to Governor Smith and the General Council. "We have 104 men and two distinct fortresses [the Alamo and San Antonio] to garrison. . . .You, doubtless, have learned that we have no provisions or clothing since Johnson and Grant left. If there has ever been a dollar here, I have no knowledge of it. The clothing sent here by the aid and patriotic exertions of the honorable council was taken from us by the arbitrary measures of Johnson and Grant, taken from men who endured all the hardships of winter and were not even sufficiently clad for summer, many of them having but one blanket and one shirt."

Messages from Lt. Col. James C. Neill, shown dictating a letter to his secretary, James Ewing, clearly informed Texian leaders of the desperate situation at the Alamo in January 1836. He was an experienced artilleryman and impressive leader who kept the Alamo defenders together.

Neill's letter ignited the conflict between Governor Smith and the General Council, which had supported the expedition that left the men at the Alamo in such a desperate situation. "You have acted in bad faith," Smith wrote to the council, "and seem determined by your acts to destroy the very institutions which you are pledged and sworn to support. . . .you are ready to sacrifice your country at the shrine of plunder." Smith declared the council "will stand adjourned" until March 1, and the council declared that Smith was no longer governor. The Texas army split into two factions. The commands under Johnson, Grant, and Fannin followed orders from the council, while General Houston and the men defending the Alamo remained loyal to Governor Smith. There were now two Texas governments and two Texas armies.

Houston, the legally appointed commander-in-chief, rode from San Felipe to Goliad to try to stop the Matamoros expedition. On January 15, he spoke to 200 volunteers, telling them that there was no hope of support from

Governor Henry Smith

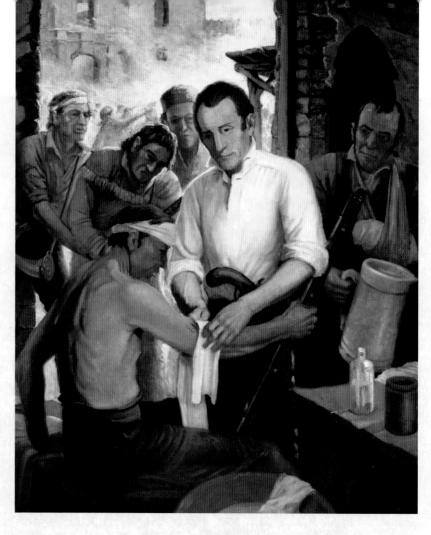

Many Alamo defenders were unable to fight because of wounds they suffered during the attack on San Antonio in December 1835, or because of illnesses from the poor food and harsh winter. Chief Surgeon Dr. Amos Pollard, shown here bandaging a wounded man, was greatly hindered by a lack of medical supplies—a situation that became much worse when Frank Johnson and James Grant took many supplies with them for the attack on Matamoros.

Mexican Federalists and that it was time to declare Texas independence. "Let us then, comrades, sever that link that binds us to that rusty chain of the Mexican Confederation; let us break off the live slab from the dying cactus that it may not dry up with the remainder; let us plant it anew that it may spring luxuriantly out of the fruitful savannah."

In the middle of Houston's speech, a messenger arrived with another note from Colonel Neill at the Alamo. Neill had received reports that there was a Mexican Army of 3,000 men at Laredo, on the Rio Grande, and 1,000 of them were heading for San Antonio, while 2,000 were bound for Matamoros. "I hope we will be re-inforced in eight days," he wrote, "or we will be overrun by the enemy, but, if I have only 100 men, I will fight 1,000 as long as I can and then not surrender."

Houston asked James Bowie, who was also at Goliad, to gather volunteers and reinforce the Alamo. Only 30 men agreed to go. Most volunteers at Goliad were recent arrivals from the United States who were more interested in plundering Mexico than in defending Texas.

Houston himself did not believe it was possible to defend the Alamo with volunteers. On the day that Bowie left, the commander-in-chief wrote to Governor Smith, "I have ordered the fortifications in the town of Béxar [San Antonio] to be demolished, and, if you think well of it, I will remove all the cannons and other munitions of war to Gonzales and Copano, blow up the Alamo and abandon the place, as it will be impossible to keep up the Station with volunteers."

Bowie and his volunteers rode 80 miles in a single day to reinforce the Alamo. They arrived to discover that out of 114 men, only 80 were healthy, and these men were evenly split between the town and old mission. A lawyer named Green B. Jameson acted as military engineer, working to strengthen the defenses. Jameson described his efforts in a letter to General Houston with a "plot" or diagram of the mission. "You can plainly see by the plot that the Alamo never was built for a military people for a fortress," he explained. Yet he believed he could make it strong enough to withstand attack, if he could take better care of the soldiers. "The men here will not labour and I cannot ask it of them until they are better clad and fed."

Governor Smith rejected Houston's suggestion to blow up the mission and decided to defend the Alamo. Bowie and Colonel Neill came to the same conclusion. For Neill, an artilleryman, the main issue was the cannons. Edwards and Grant had taken many mules and horses, so there were not enough work animals in San Antonio to haul the cannons away. "If teams could be obtained here by any means to remove the Cannons and Public Property," he wrote, "I would immediately destroy the fortifications and abandon the place."

For Bowie, protecting San Antonio was more personal. In 1831, he had married Ursula Veramendi, the daughter of one of San Antonio's most wealthy and powerful Tejano families. Tragically, Bowie lost his young wife in a cholera epidemic two years later, but he still had many relatives and friends among the Tejano community. On February 2, after two weeks of examining the situation in San Antonio and the Alamo, he wrote to Governor Smith:

This Scottish-made Spanish cannon, 1 of 21 cannons at the Alamo, was probably used on the west wall facing San Antonio.

"Relief at this post, in men, money, & provisions is of vital importance & is wanted instantly. . . .The salvation of Texas depends in great measure in keeping Béjar out of the hands of the enemy. It serves as the frontier picquet guard and if it were in the possession of Santa Anna there is no strong hold from which to repell him in his march [across Texas]. . . .Col. Neill & Myself have come to the solemn resolution that we will rather die in these ditches than give it up to the enemy. These citizens deserve our protection and the public safety demands our lives rather than to evacuate this post to the enemy."

Even before receiving Bowie's plea, Governor Smith had ordered William B. Travis—who now had a Texas army commission as a lieutenant colonel—to raise a company of cavalry and ride to San Antonio. Although he had orders to enlist 100 men, Travis was only able to assemble 30, and he blamed the conflicts among Texas leaders for his difficulties. "The people are cold & indifferent," he wrote to Smith. "They are worn down & exhausted with the war, & in consequence of dissentions between contending & rival chieftains, they have lost all confidence in their own Govt. and officers." On February 3, the day after Bowie's letter, Travis arrived at the Alamo accompanied by his slave, Joe. The rest of Travis's men followed two days later.

Another small group also arrived at this time, led by David Crockett, a former U.S. Congressman from Tennessee. Crockett was famous throughout America because of several books and a play based on his adventures on the frontier. Although he only brought a dozen men, Crockett's arrival boosted the morale of the Alamo defenders. In one of San Antonio's public squares, the famous man got up on a packing crate and gave a speech to the soldiers and townspeople:

"Fellow citizens, I am among you. I have come to your country, though not I hope, through any selfish motive whatever. I have come to aid you all that I can in your noble cause. I shall identify myself with your interests, and all the honor that I desire is that of defending, as a high private, in common with my fellow-citizens, the liberties of our common country."

On the night of February 10, the citizens of San Antonio held a dance, called a fandango, in Crockett's honor. A Tejano friend of Bowie, Antonio Menchaca,

David Crockett

The fandango, a popular form of entertainment and socializing in San Antonio, is portrayed in this painting by Theodore Gentilz.

later recalled, "While at the ball, at about 1 o'clock, A.M. of the 11th, a courier, sent by [Tejano leader] Plácido Benavides, arrived . . . with the intelligence that Santa Ana, was starting from the Presidio [del] Rio Grande, with 13,000 troops, 10,000 Infantry and 3,000 Cavalry, with the view of taking San Antonio."

Menchaca or the courier may have exaggerated the numbers. Santa Anna's army was about 6,000 strong, and they were spread out for miles on both sides of the Rio Grande. However, the basic information in this report was absolutely correct. There was a large army on the move headed straight for San Antonio.

Antonio Menchaca

The courier asked to speak to Juan Seguín, but Seguín was not there. So he showed the letter to Menchaca, who shared it with Bowie. Travis was nearby, and Bowie called to him to read the letter. "Travis said that at that moment he could not stay to read letters," Menchaca remembered, "for he was dancing with the most beautiful lady in San Antonio. Bowie told him that the letter was one of grave importance, and for him to leave his partner. Travis came and brought Crockett with him. Travis and Bowie understood Spanish, Crockett did not."

The letter was dated four days earlier, and according to Menchaca, Travis said, "It will take 13,000 men from the Presidio [del] Rio Grande to this place thirteen or fourteen days to get here; this is the 4th day. Let us dance to-night and to-morrow we will make provisions for our defense."

On the nights of February 25 and 26, some Alamo defenders snuck out of the fort to set fire to a nearby group of small houses called *jacales*, which had given cover to the Mexican soldiers. In the foreground, a Texian pours gunpowder into his rifle while another fires his musket.

the siege

On February 11, the day after the fandango, Colonel James Neill left the Alamo because of sickness in his family. Neill was a remarkable officer who had held the men together without enough food, clothing, or money. James Bowie, a strong leader himself, wrote of the Alamo commander: "I cannot eulogise [praise] the conduct & character of Col Neill too highly: no other man in the army could have kept men at this post, under the neglect they have experienced."

Neill left Travis in command, since he was the next ranking officer with a regular Army commission. The veterans who had stayed after conquering San Antonio were mostly volunteers rather than regular army soldiers, and they preferred taking orders from James Bowie, an older, more experienced colonel of volunteers who had proven himself in the Battle for San Antonio. After a brief but bitter conflict, the two officers reached a compromise: Travis would command the regular Texas army soldiers and the volunteer cavalry; Bowie would command the rest of the volunteers.

On February 14, the co-commanders wrote to Governor Smith informing him of their agreement. The real purpose of the letter, however, was to ask for money to pay their men. "It is useless to talk of Keeping up this Garrison any longer without money, as we believe that unless we receive some shortly, the men will all leave.—From all the information we have received, there is no doubt but that the enemy will shortly advance upon this place & that this will be the first point of attack."

Travis and Bowie may have had their disagreements, but they were right about this. Two days later, General Santa Anna crossed the Rio Grande with an escort of 50 soldiers. His advance army of 1,500 men was already ahead of him on the road to San Antonio, while thousands more trailed behind. At the same time, a smaller army of about 550 men under General José Urrea, marched east toward Matamoros, with orders to prevent any attack there and then swing

General José Urrea

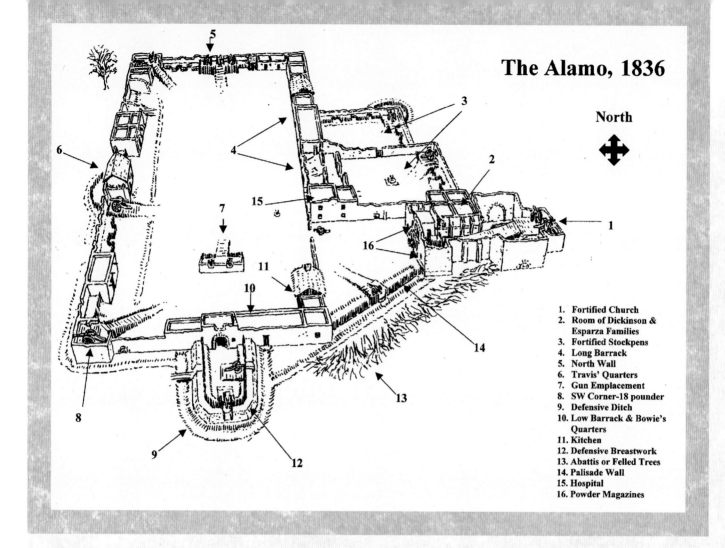

The Alamo, 1836

North

1. Fortified Church
2. Room of Dickinson & Esparza Families
3. Fortified Stockpens
4. Long Barrack
5. North Wall
6. Travis' Quarters
7. Gun Emplacement
8. SW Corner-18 pounder
9. Defensive Ditch
10. Low Barrack & Bowie's Quarters
11. Kitchen
12. Defensive Breastwork
13. Abattis or Felled Trees
14. Palisade Wall
15. Hospital
16. Powder Magazines

Originally built as a mission, the Alamo was made into a reasonable fortress first by Mexican soldiers under General Cos and then by the Texians and Tejanos. The size of the compound (three acres) made it difficult to defend. The Texians did not have enough men to defend the walls in close formation while also properly manning the cannons, which each required five or six men to keep them firing.

north into Texas and take the fortress at Goliad. After Santa Anna took back the Alamo, the two armies would either meet or squeeze the Texians between them.

For the next week, Travis and Bowie supervised efforts to strengthen the Alamo and prepare for attack. The men dug ditches, fortified the walls, and mounted cannons under the direction of Major Jameson. There were 21 cannons in all, 18 in working order, along with hundreds of Mexican muskets and thousands of cartridges left behind by General Cos's men. There were so many guns that each Texian could have four or five, loaded and ready at all times. That was the good news. The bad news was that the Mexican gunpowder was of poor quality, and there was not enough good powder and ammunition for the cannons.

Day after day, Travis sent out pleas for help, but no help arrived. The Texas government and Texas army had fallen apart. Governor Smith and the council were still at odds, looking toward a convention on March 1 that would create a new government. Sam Houston was out of Texas for most of February, on orders from Smith to meet with the Cherokee Indians and ensure that they would not join the Mexicans in the coming battles. Houston was successful in his mission, but it was a bad time for the commander-in-chief to be away.

On February 22, the Texians and Tejanos held another fandango in San Antonio to celebrate the birthday of George Washington. It was a strange moment: Mexicans and Americans—many of them Mexican citizens—dancing together to honor an American president as the Mexican president was coming to attack them. It was also foolish and defiant. Travis and Bowie had received many reports from Tejano scouts regarding the approach of Santa Anna's army, and they knew it was very near.

The next morning, February 23, Travis—who was staying in town—woke up to the sounds of Tejanos leaving San Antonio. Dr. John Sutherland remembered, "The citizens of every class were hurrying to and fro, through the streets, with obvious signs of excitement. Houses were being emptied, and their contents put into carts, and hauled off. Such of the poorer class, who had no better mode of conveyance, were shouldering their effects, and leaving on foot."

Dr. John Sutherland

Travis posted a man in the bell tower of the Cathedral of San Fernando, the highest point in San Antonio, with orders to ring the bell if he saw anything. Early that afternoon, the sentinel rang the bell and shouted, "The enemy are in view!" Several men scrambled up but could see nothing. The sentinel swore he had seen the army.

On orders from Travis, Sutherland and another American named John Smith, who had lived in San Antonio for nine years and knew the countryside, rode out about a mile and a half west of town. They found themselves "within one hundred and fifty yards of fifteen hundred men, well mounted and equipped. Their polished armor glistening in the rays of the sun, as they were formed in a line, behind the chaparral and mezquite bushes."

Sutherland and Smith rode quickly back to town, but the road was muddy from recent rains, and Sutherland's horse slipped and fell, injuring one of the doctor's knees. With Smith's help, horse and rider both got up again, and they continued on to find David Crockett, mounted on his horse and heading for the Alamo. Crockett informed them that Travis had seen enough to know the enemy was on its way and had moved himself and his men into the old mission.

Captain Juan Seguín and his Tejano volunteers headed for the Alamo as well. Seguín remembered that as they marched down one of San Antonio's main streets, "the ladies exclaimed 'Poor fellows you will all be killed, what shall we do?'"

One of Seguín's men, Gregorio Esparza—whose brother had fought under General Cos during the Battle of Béxar—brought his wife and five children into the mission. Their oldest son, Enrique, just eight years old at the time, remembered, "It took the whole day to move, and an hour before sundown we were inside the fort. There was a bridge over the river. . .and just as we got to it we could hear Santa Anna's drums beating" in the heart of San Antonio.

There were other civilians, too, more than 20 in all, including James Bowie's sister-in-law, Juana Alsbury, her baby son, Aleto, and her sister Gertrudis. One Texian officer, Captain Almeron Dickinson, also brought his young wife, Susanna, and their 14-month-old daughter, Angelina, with him into the Alamo.

There was little food inside the Alamo compound, but the men found 30 head of cattle wandering through San Antonio just as the defenders were heading for the mission. Bowie and others broke into a group of deserted houses and found almost 90 bushels of corn. To Travis, it seemed that these two finds were evidence that "The Lord is on our side." In truth, it only meant that they would not starve to death.

Santa Anna arrived late that afternoon, and the Mexican Army raised a blood red flag to the top of the Cathedral, which Travis rightly interpreted to mean "no quarter"—no paroles, no mercy, no prisoners. He answered with a booming shot from his largest cannon, mounted at the

The Esparza family heads for the Alamo. Only one child is shown, but Enrique later remembered that "my elder sister, myself and three younger brothers, one a baby in arms" entered the fortress.

Travis leans on the west wall after ordering his largest cannon—an 18-pounder (meaning it could shoot an 18-pound ball)—fired at San Antonio in reply to Santa Anna's demand for surrender. The blast blows off the hat of Travis's slave, Joe.

southwest corner of the Alamo compound and aimed at the city. The Mexicans replied with four shots from their howitzers, small cannons that could lob explosive shells over the Alamo walls.

There was a break in the firing, and—though they had agreed to work together—Bowie and Travis each sent out separate messengers with notes asking to explain the conditions of the siege. Santa Anna's reply was clear:

"The Mexican army cannot come to terms under any conditions with rebellious foreigners to whom there is no other recourse left, if they wish to save their lives, than to place themselves immediately at the disposal of the Supreme Government." Although Santa Anna promised the possibility of "clemency" or mercy "after some considerations are taken up," the Alamo defenders were not willing to place their lives at the "disposal" of General Santa Anna. They voted to stay and fight, and Travis ordered another booming shot from his biggest cannon.

The next day, James Bowie turned over full command of the Alamo to William Travis. Bowie had been feeling poorly for some time, and he was now so sick that he could barely take care of himself, let alone lead others. He was moved into a small room near the Alamo gate, where Juana Alsbury and her sister Gertrudis helped care for him. The Mexican cannon fire began again in the afternoon, pounding the fort relentlessly. That evening, Travis sat down in his own quarters to write the most famous letter of the Texas Revolution:

Lieutenant Colonel William B. Travis

"To the People of Texas & all Americans <u>in the world</u>—Fellow citizens & compatriots—I am besieged, by a thousand or more of the Mexicans under Santa Anna—I have sustained a continual Bombardment & cannonade for 24 hours & have not lost a man—the enemy has demanded a surrender at discretion, otherwise, the garrison are to be put to the sword, if the fort is taken—I have answered the demand with a cannon shot, & our flag still waves proudly from the walls—<u>I shall never surrender or retreat. Then,</u> I call on you in the name of Liberty, of patriotism & every thing dear to the American character, to come to our aid, with all dispatch—The enemy is receiving reinforcements daily & will no doubt increase to three or four thousand in four or five days. If this call is neglected, I am determined to sustain myself as long as possible & die like a soldier who never forgets what is due to his own honor & that of his country—<u>Victory or Death</u>"

Travis's message was carried to Gonzales by Captain Albert Martin, and then on to San Felipe by another courier named Launcelot Smither. Two hundred copies of the message were quickly printed, and it later appeared in Texas newspapers. Some reinforcements did prepare for action, but response was slow.

In San Antonio, the Mexican cannons continued to pound the Alamo, and the Mexican Army moved into position to build fortifications and surround the fort. Travis sent out several small parties to harass the Mexicans and fired his cannons only when necessary, for there wasn't enough gunpowder to be careless. Texian sharpshooters with their Kentucky hunting rifles killed a number of soldiers from long range. According to local Tejanos, Santa Anna himself got a little too close while inspecting his fortifications, and David Crockett barely missed him with a bullet from 200 yards.

There was a major skirmish on February 25, and Juan Seguín left the Alamo that night, carrying a message from Travis to Sam Houston. "Do hasten on aid to me as rapidly as possible," Travis wrote, ". . .it will be impossible for us to keep them out much longer. If they overpower us, we fall a sacrifice at the shrine of our country." Travis was a desperate man in a desperate situation, and he never would have guessed that Houston would think he was exaggerating the threat. Yet that was exactly the case.

By February 29, Houston was back from his mission to the Cherokee, preparing for the convention to begin the next day in the town of Washington-on-the-Brazos. According to an eyewitness, he convinced a number of people there that "a fraud had been practiced upon the people by the officers of the frontier, for party purposes; that there was not an enemy on our borders." Houston had been so disturbed by the earlier political conflicts that he now believed that both Travis and Fannin—who was holding down the presidio at Goliad—were exaggerating the threat because they wanted his job as commander-in-chief. It was a ridiculous idea. Travis was just trying to survive at the Alamo, while Fannin begged the General Council to relieve him. "I am a better judge of my military abilities than others," he wrote, "and if I am qualified to command an Army, I have not found it out."

Qualified or not, James Fannin commanded more than 400 men at Goliad, the largest concentration of Texian troops. Travis and Bowie had written to him the day that Santa Anna arrived, and on February 26—the day after Travis wrote his letter to Houston—Fannin set out with 320 men and four cannons

On the morning of February 25, defenders fighting from trenches outside the Alamo (below) fire at Mexican soldiers who had crossed the river and occupied a settlement called La Villita (The Little Village) "within point blank shot" of the Alamo's southern wall. Travis wrote, "The Hon. David Crockett was seen at all points, animating the men to do their duty."

to reinforce the Alamo. His men struggled to cross the rain-swollen San Antonio River and then lost their oxen on the other side, leaving them with the prospect of an 80-mile march without enough food or ammunition.

By this time, they also had word that General Urrea's army was approaching from the south, so Fannin and his officers decided to return to Goliad and defend the presidio. "It is now obvious that the Enemy have entered Texas at two points," Fannin wrote in explaining his action, "for the purpose of attacking Bexar & this place—The first has been attacked and we may expect the enemy here momentarily—Both places are important."

Fannin has been criticized for not reinforcing the Alamo, but he was right: The Alamo and the presidio at Goliad were equally important. General Urrea's small army moved quickly and efficiently. On February 27, he attacked 40 Texians under Frank Johnson in the town of San Patricio, killing 10, capturing 18, and scattering the others. They turned south to pursue what was left of the Matamoros expedition under Dr. James Grant. They would destroy this small force a few days later. For the moment, Goliad was safe, but Urrea would return.

Colonel James Fannin

At the Alamo, a small group of reinforcements finally arrived at 3 a.m. on March 1, when 32 men from Gonzales rode into the Alamo compound. Around this same time, however, many Tejanos decided to leave. According to some accounts, Santa Anna made an offer that they would be given amnesty, but other accounts suggest the opposite—that Santa Anna had even greater punishment in mind for the Tejanos, whom he considered traitors. In either case, the fact that Tejano leader Juan Seguín had left to deliver Travis's message to Houston played a part in the men's decisions. Among those who remained was Gregorio Esparza, who stayed on with his family.

Travis wrote several letters on March 3, and his couriers were still able to carry them through the Mexican lines. One letter was addressed to his close friend Jesse Grimes, a delegate to the Convention at Washington-on-the-Brazos. Grimes's 19-year-old son, Alfred, was among Travis's soldiers. After describing how they had survived "a shower of bombs and cannon balls" without losing a man, Travis made a final plea:

James Bonham, who had been sent to get reinforcements, returns on March 3 with a letter from Three-Legged Willie Williamson indicating that 60 men are on their way from Gonzales, 300 more from other areas, and that Fannin is coming with 300 men and 4 pieces of artillery. Unfortunately, Fannin and the other large group never made it, though it's possible that betweem 50 and 60 men did arrive on the 4th. Bonham would die with the others at the Alamo.

"Let the Convention go on and make a declaration of independence; and we will then understand and the world will understand what we are fighting for. If independence is not declared, I shall lay down my arms and so will the men under my command. But under the flag of independence, we are ready to peril our lives a hundred times a day, and to dare the monster who is fighting us under a blood-red flag, threatening to murder all prisoners and to make Texas a waste desert. . . . if my countrymen do not rally to my relief, I am determined to perish in the defense of this place, and my bones shall reproach my country for her neglect."

In his many letters from the Alamo, this was the only time Travis even mentioned the possibility of surrender. He knew that surrender was not a real option, because he was right that Santa Anna would take no prisoners. What he did not know—what he and his men would never know—was that the convention had formally declared the independence of Texas from Mexico the day before.

"Siege of the Alamo," by Lajos Markos, captures the intensity of the battle as Mexican soldiers swarm over the walls. "The most daring of our veterans tried to be the first to climb," wrote one Mexican officer, ". . .yelling wildly so that room could be made for them, at times climbing over their own comrades."

46

the battle

The 32 men from Gonzales are the last reinforcements that we know for certain reached the Alamo. New evidence suggests that between 50 and 60 men— possibly guided by David Crockett—may have slipped through the Mexican lines on the morning of March 4. If so, this brought the number of defenders to 250 or 260, though not all were healthy enough to fight. Santa Anna had definitely received reinforcements. About 830 Mexican soldiers had arrived on March 3, bringing the total in San Antonio to almost 2,400 with many more on the way.

That afternoon, Santa Anna called his top officers together to discuss attacking the Alamo. According to Colonel Almonte, who was at the meeting, several officers wanted to wait until two large cannons arrived so that they could smash through the north wall of the fortress. Among these was General Cos, who had rejoined the army during its march toward Texas and knew the Alamo better than the other officers. The large cannons were expected to arrive in three days, but Santa Anna did not want to wait, and he did not think they would be necessary.

No decision was made at this meeting. Then at 2 p.m. on the following day, General Santa Anna issued orders that the army would attack in the early morning darkness of Sunday, March 6. Because he would not wait for the big cannons, his soldiers would use ladders to climb the walls—which guaranteed death for those in front. Several officers objected to this strategy, and there are stories about Santa Anna's disregard for his men. Captain Fernando Urissa reported that the general held up a piece of chicken he was eating and said: "What are the lives of soldiers more than of so many chickens? I tell you, the Alamo must fall, and my orders must be obeyed at all hazards. If our soldiers are driven back, the next line in their rear must force those before them forward, and compel them to scale the walls, cost what it may."

The main attack force would be composed of 1,100 men in four columns, who would attack at different points along the Alamo walls. Another 400 men would be ready to fight but held in reserve, commanded directly by Santa Anna. The cavalry, about 300 men armed with long lances, would wait just south of the Alamo "to scout the country, to prevent the possibility of escape." That possibility was escape not only by the defenders but also by the Mexican soldiers, many of whom were new recruits who had never been tested in battle.

"The Commanding Officers will see that the men have the chin-straps of their caps down, and that they wear either shoes or sandals," read the official order. "The troops composing the columns of attack will turn in to sleep at dark, to be in readiness to move at 12 o'clock at night. . . .The arms, principally the bayonets, should be in perfect order. . . .The honor of the nation being interested in this engagement against the bold and lawless foreigners who are opposing us, His Excellency expects that every man will do his

According to one famous legend, Travis drew a line in the dirt and asked all who would stay and fight to step over the line. Everyone crossed except a Frenchman named Louis Rose, who escaped to tell the tale. This story is based on a report in 1873 from William Zuber, who said his parents heard it from Rose and later told it to him. As with many Alamo legends, the truth is questionable, but there is no question regarding the bravery of the Alamo defenders.

duty, and exert himself to give a day of glory to the country."

Later that afternoon, Santa Anna ordered his cannons to stop firing at the Alamo. He knew the men inside were exhausted and hoped that they would go to sleep so his soldiers could surprise them in the night. The men did sleep that night, and for most of them it must have been a strange and fitful rest.

They were not professional soldiers; they were shopkeepers, blacksmiths, lawyers, doctors, farmers, and one famous congressman from Tennessee. They came from 20 states and 6 foreign countries. They ranged in age from 15 to 56. Some knew each other before they arrived; others were total strangers united by a shared belief in their cause. For some it had begun as Mexican citizens fighting for the Constitution of 1824, but that idea had been left behind.

In early February, the Alamo defenders had elected two representatives to the Convention at Washington-on-the-Brazos. According to Green B. Jameson, the men they chose were "staunch independence men & damn any other than such." Since that time, many defenders had come and gone, but it's safe to say that nearly every man in the Alamo compound on March 5 shared Jameson's point of view. They didn't know about the Texas Declaration of Independence, but they knew what they were fighting for: a free and independent Texas.

As ordered, the Mexican soldiers were awakened at midnight and began to move into their positions around 1 a.m. The night was cold, but Santa Anna had ordered that "the men will wear neither overcoats nor blankets, or anything that may impede the rapidity of their motions." So they shivered in the darkness, thinking of the battle to come.

At 5:30 a.m., Santa Anna gave the order to attack. The four columns of infantry moved quickly and quietly toward their assigned points of attack. In order to avenge his earlier defeat, General Cos had the "honor" of leading the first column toward the northwest corner of the fortress. The second column headed for the north wall at a place that had been broken by earlier cannon fire and quickly patched. The third column circled to the rear of the fort to

Two companies of volunteers from New Orleans—called the New Orleans Grays for the color of their uniforms—joined the Texians in time to fight in the first battle for San Antonio. Although most of the Grays left to join the ill-fated Matamoros expedition, this flag was captured at the Alamo and sent back to Mexico City by Santa Anna to "show plainly the true intention of the treacherous colonists, and of their abettors, who came from the ports of the United States of the North."

Enrique Esparza

attack the east wall, while the fourth column headed for the south end of the compound, near the church, where there was no wall at all but rather a defense made of trees laid on their sides (see diagram, page 38).

Travis had posted sentries outside the fort, but the Mexican soldiers killed them before they could give the alarm. The attack might have been a total surprise except that a soldier somewhere in the ranks shouted *"Viva Santa Anna!"* (Long live Santa Anna!) Another soldier replied, *"Viva La Republica!"* (Long live the Republic!) Suddenly hundreds of Mexican voices were shouting in the dark.

Adjutant John Baugh, the Texian officer on duty that night, ran quickly across the compound, shouting, "Colonel Travis, the Mexicans are coming!"

Travis and his slave, Joe, were asleep in Travis's quarters. Joe remembered that the two of them grabbed their guns and ran toward the north wall, with Travis shouting, "Come on, boys, the Mexicans are upon us, and we'll give them *Hell.*"

Other defenders scrambled into their assigned positions. Gregorio Esparza was sleeping with his wife and children in a room within the Alamo church. His son Enrique remembered, ". . .there was a great shooting and firing at the northwest corner of the fort, and I heard my mother say: 'Gregorio, the soldiers have jumped the wall. The fight's begun.' He got up and picked up his arms and went into the fight. I never saw him again."

In fact, the Mexican soldiers had not yet climbed the walls, and the "great shooting and firing" that Enrique heard was the booming of Texian cannons driving off the first wave of the attack. One soldier with Cos's column recalled, "We suffered two cannon volleys of grapeshot that felled more than forty men. The tenacious resistance of our enemies was amazing." Colonel José de la Peña, attacking with the second column at the north wall, wrote that "a single cannon volley did away with half the company of chasseurs [infantry] from [the city of] Toluca."

Twice the Alamo defenders drove the Mexican soldiers back, with heavy losses. The first three columns swarmed together beneath the north wall. "All united at one point," wrote de la Peña, "mixing and forming a confused mass."

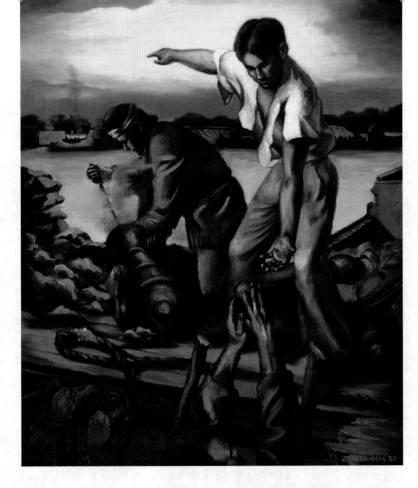

Gregorio Esparza (wearing headband) prepares his cannon to fire another shot from atop the Alamo church. Gregorio's brother, Francisco, who was in the Mexican Army but did not take part in the battle, later testified: "I proceeded to the Alamo and found the dead body of my Brother in one of the Rooms of the Alamo, he had received a ball in his breast and a stab from a Sword in his side."

Disgusted with the lack of progress, Santa Anna threw his reserves into the battle, adding another 400 men to the "confused mass" at the north wall. Standing atop the wall, Travis fired his double-barrel shotgun at the attackers and received a single fatal shot to the forehead, falling across a cannon. Joe ran through the courtyard and hid in one of the buildings, as the Mexican soldiers began to swarm over the walls.

By this time, the soldiers had regained some order and returned to their original objectives. The reserves and second column scaled the north wall, while General Cos's men climbed the west wall, and the third column scrambled over the lower walls to the east. The fourth column entered in the southwest corner, where they took control of the largest cannon and turned it on the defenders.

In the roofless Alamo church, Captain Almeron Dickinson stood beside a smaller cannon on an earthen ramp that gave him a clear view of the crumbling defenses. He ran down the ramp to where his 22-year-old wife, Susanna, and their 14-month-old daughter, Angelina, were hiding and exclaimed, "Great God Sue, the Mexicans are inside our walls! All is lost! If they spare you, save my child."

Susanna Dickinson

"Then, with a parting kiss," Mrs. Dickinson remembered, "he drew his sword and plunged into the strife, then raging in different portions of the fortifications."

The "strife" raged everywhere throughout the Alamo compound, where the defenders had withdrawn from the walls and taken refuge in various buildings, fighting to the end. There was now some pre-dawn light, but there was so much smoke from gunpowder that neither attacker nor defender could clearly see. Mexican Sergeant Francisco Becerra provided a vivid description of the final fighting:

"Our troops, inspirited by success, continued the attack with energy and boldness. The Texians fought like devils. It was at short range—muzzle to muzzle—hand to hand—musket and rifle—bayonet and Bowie knife—all were mingled in confusion. Here a squad of Mexicans, there a Texian or two. The crash of firearms, the shouts of defiance, the cries of the dying and the wounded, made a din almost infernal. The Texians defended desperately every inch of the fort—overpowered by numbers, they would be forced to abandon a room; they would rally in the next, and defend it until further resistance became impossible."

It was over before sunrise. Colonel Almonte, usually accurate with times

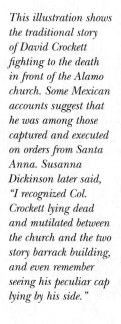

This illustration shows the traditional story of David Crockett fighting to the death in front of the Alamo church. Some Mexican accounts suggest that he was among those captured and executed on orders from Santa Anna. Susanna Dickinson later said, "I recognized Col. Crockett lying dead and mutilated between the church and the two story barrack building, and even remember seeing his peculiar cap lying by his side."

and other data, wrote, "At 5 A.M., the columns were posted at their respective stations, and at half past 5 the attack or assault was made, and continued until 6 A.M. when the enemy attempted in vain to fly, but they were overtaken and put to the sword. . . ."

If this is true, the entire battle lasted 30 minutes. However, Almonte's reference to the enemy attempting "in vain to fly" may refer to the retreat of the Texians from the walls into the Alamo compound. It also may refer to a group of Texians who tried to escape only to be killed by the Mexican cavalry with their long, sharp lances. In any case, the battle was brief, 30 to 90 minutes.

When the fighting was over, Santa Anna entered the fort with his staff officers who had not participated in the battle. According to Colonel de la Peña, seven Texians had been captured and were brought before Santa Anna "under the protection of General Castrillón," a Mexican commander who believed in "civilized" warfare. When General Castrillón asked that the men be shown mercy, Santa Anna turned his back and ordered them executed. The officers who had fought refused to obey his order, but some of his aides "thrust themselves forward, in order to flatter their commander, and with swords in hand, fell upon these unfortunate, defenseless men just as a tiger leaps upon his prey."

Francisco Ruiz

De la Peña's account is controversial, but some executions probably did take place. Santa Anna had made it clear that there would be no prisoners.

As commanding general and Mexican president, Santa Anna was especially interested in the rebel leaders, so he asked the alcalde of San Antonio, Francisco Ruiz, to identify the bodies of the three colonels—Travis, Bowie, and Crockett (who had been elected colonel in the Tennessee militia). "On the north battery of the fortress lay the lifeless body of Col. Travis," Ruiz recalled, "on the gun-carriage, shot *only* in the forehead. Toward the west. . .we found the body of Col. Crockett. Col. Bowie was found dead in his bed, in one of the rooms of the south side."

That morning, Santa Anna dictated a report to the government in Mexico City. "Victory belongs to the army, which, at this very moment, 8 o'clock A.M., achieved a complete and glorious triumph that will render its memory imperishable."

In this report, Santa Anna greatly exaggerated the number of Alamo defenders as 600; the true count was less than half that, between 180 and 260. He also greatly underestimated his own losses at 70 dead and 300 wounded. The true count was higher, hundreds perhaps, and many of the wounded would later die of their wounds. "The cause for which they fell," Santa Anna claimed, "renders their loss less painful, as it is the duty of the Mexican soldiers to die for the defence of the rights of the nation; and all of us were ready for any sacrifice to promote this fond object; nor will we, hereafter, suffer any foreigners, whatever their origin may be, to insult our country and to pollute its soil."

Around the time that Santa Anna dictated this report, Captain Urissa, who earlier had heard the general comparing his soldiers to chickens, entered the compound and found Santa Anna standing among the dead bodies. "As I bowed, he said to me, pointing to the dead: 'These are the chickens. Much blood has been shed; but the battle is over: it was but a small affair.'"

That afternoon, on orders from Santa Anna, Francisco Ruiz supervised the burning of the dead bodies of Alamo defenders. "About 3 o'clock in the afternoon they commenced laying the wood and dry branches, upon which a file of dead bodies was placed; more wood was piled on them, and another file

brought, and in this manner they were all arranged in layers. Kindling wood was distributed through the pile, and about 5 o'clock in the evening it was lighted."

Ruiz counted 182 bodies. One defender—Gregorio Esparza—was buried in the San Antonio cemetery, because his brother, a Mexican soldier, obtained special permission from General Cos. For this reason, 183 is the traditional number given for the Alamo defenders, but there may have been more who were killed outside the fort and were left where they lay. The total was nearer 200 or 250 if the second group of reinforcements arrived.

Whatever the number, one fact is certain: A small group of brave defenders, outnumbered almost ten to one, had made Santa Anna's army pay for the Alamo in blood. "The gallantry of the few Texians who defended the Alamo was really wondered at by the Mexican army," Ruiz recalled. "Even the Generals were astonished at their vigorous resistance, and how dearly victory had been bought."

General Santa Anna, in white pants and blue jacket, is presented to a wounded General Houston after the Battle of San Jacinto. Colonel Almonte, dressed in an officer's uniform, serves as interpreter, while Erasmus "Deaf" Smith–whose daring helped secure the Texians' victory–cups his ear to listen.

On the day the Alamo fell, Sam Houston left the Convention at Washington-on-the-Brazos to take command of a new Texas army gathering at Gonzales. He moved slowly, taking five days for a two-day trip; he still did not believe that Santa Anna's army was in San Antonio. Houston discovered the terrible truth on March 11, when Susanna Dickinson and her child arrived in Gonzales, along with Travis's slave, Joe, and Ben, the black American cook of Colonel Almonte. Houston and Susanna Dickinson cried together as she told him the story.

Houston ordered the town of Gonzales burned to keep it from being occupied by the enemy and led his army and the settlers on a long, muddy retreat into eastern Texas, pursued by a part of Santa Anna's army. Colonel Fannin's men were supposed to join Houston's force, but Fannin also moved slowly. On March 19, he left Goliad, only to be surprised by Mexican cavalry under General Urrea. Although they inflicted heavy casualties on the Mexicans, Fannin's men surrendered the following morning and were taken back to the fortress at Goliad. On March 27, some 342 prisoners, including James Fannin, were executed on orders from Santa Anna.

On the afternoon of April 21, Houston's army of about 900 men attacked almost 1,400 Mexican soldiers under Santa Anna and General Cos along the San Jacinto River—just a few hundred yards from Lynch's Ferry, where Travis and his men had set out to attack Anahuac ten months earlier.

Santa Anna was so confident that he and his men took an afternoon siesta, and he did not post sentries. With cries of "Remember the Alamo! Remember Goliad!" Houston's army overran the Mexican camp in 18 minutes. The killing lasted longer, as Texians slaughtered fleeing soldiers in vengeance for the Alamo and Goliad. About 630 Mexican soldiers were killed and 730 captured, including 200 wounded. According to Houston, the Texian losses were "two killed and twenty-three wounded, six of whom mortally."

Santa Anna was captured the next day, disguised as a common soldier. Although the Texians shouted for the dictator's death, Houston knew he would be more valuable alive. There were still thousands of Mexican soldiers in Texas, and Houston offered Santa Anna his life in return for withdrawing all Mexican forces. Santa Anna agreed.

Texas was an independent republic for the next nine years. It was annexed by the United States in 1845. Mexico's refusal to officially recognize Texas independence would lead to the Mexican War in 1846.

TIME LINE OF TEXAS AND THE AMERICAN SOUTHWEST 1528-1853

All of the land that is now the American Southwest and Mexico was once claimed by Spain. In 1821 when Mexico won independence from Spain, this land became part of the Republic of Mexico. Although this time line provides some key points on early Spanish movement into other areas of the Southwest, the primary focus is on Texas under Spain and Mexico, as an independent Republic, and in the early years of U.S. statehood.

Unlike Spain, which tried to keep Americans out of its territory, Mexico was eager to trade with its northern neighbor. Mexicans welcomed American traders into Santa Fe along the famous Santa Fe Trail. As you have read in this book, they also welcomed Americans to settle in Texas. This partnership between the two new nations of North America was promising at first. However, Mexico's internal conflicts, combined with American hunger for land, ultimately led to the Texas Revolution.

Mexico did not officially recognize Texas independence after the revolution, and there was an ongoing conflict over the border (see disputed area on the map below). When Texas became part of the United States in 1845, this border dispute became a conflict between two nations, leading directly to the Mexican War of 1846-48. By winning the war, the United States secured almost the entire Southwest and parts of states in neighboring regions. The Gadsden Purchase in 1853 (see time line) completed U.S. acquisition of the American Southwest.

Spanish Period ⊕ 1528-1821

1528
A Spanish expedition is shipwrecked on Galveston Island off the Gulf Coast of present-day Texas. Four survivors, led by Alvar Nuñez Cabeza de Vaca, ultimately walk to the Pacific coast of Mexico. They arrive in 1534 with tales of golden cities to the north, in what is now New Mexico.

1540
A Spanish expedition under Francisco Vásquez de Coronado enters present-day New Mexico, battles the Pueblo Indians, and explores parts of what is now the American Southwest, including the Texas panhandle.

1598 A large Spanish expedition under Juan de Oñate, including soldiers and settlers, forcibly settle among the Pueblo in New Mexico.

1680
Led by a medicine man named Popé, the Pueblo revolt and drive the Spanish out of New Mexico.

1690
Two Franciscan missions are established among Caddo Indians on the Trinity River in present-day Texas. They are abandoned in 1693.

1691
Jesuit Missionary Eusebio Kino begins working among Pima Indians in what is now southern Arizona.

1693
The Spanish return to New Mexico.

1716
Six missions are established among the Caddo in eastern Texas and Louisiana include Spanish soldiers, women, and children. The missions are abandoned in 1719.

1718
Mission of San Antonio de Valero is established, along with the Presidio and Villa of Béxar (present-day San Antonio). It is the first of five missions in the area.

1731
Sixteen Spanish families with 56 people arrive in San Antonio from the Canary Islands. They establish the new Villa of San Fernando and the first civil government (non-military/religious) in Texas.

1769
San Diego mission is established, the first of 21 missions in what is now the state of California.

1803
Louisiana Purchase gives the United States a vast region to the north and east of Spanish territory. The border between American Louisiana and Spanish Texas is in dispute.

1810
A revolt against Spanish rule, led by Father Miguel Hidalgo, erupts in Mexico. The fighting lasts 11 years.

1812-13
An "army" made up mostly of Anglo-Americans but led by a wealthy Mexican landowner, invades Texas, takes control of San Antonio, and declares a "Republic of Texas." It is defeated by Spanish soldiers.

1819
The border between the United States and Spanish territory is settled in the Adams-Onis Treaty. Spain gives Florida to the United States, and the United States gives up all claims to Texas. That same year another group of Americans and Mexicans invades Texas and declares a Republic, but they are driven out by Spanish soldiers.

1820
Moses Austin arrives in San Antonio and receives a grant of 200,000 acres of land to bring 300 colonists into Spanish Texas.

Mexican Period ⊕ 1821-1836

1821
Mexico, led by former Spanish Army officer Augustin de Iturbide, wins independence from Spain. Stephen F. Austin, Moses's son, leads a small group of colonists to begin settling his father's land grant. Missouri businessman William Becknell transports American goods from St. Louis to Santa Fe, opening the Santa Fe Trail.

1822
Iturbide is crowned Emperor of Mexico.

1823
Iturbide officially approves Austin's land grant in February. The following month, Iturbide is forced to give up his "throne" by forces led by Antonio López de Santa Anna. The conflict between Federalists and Centralists begins.

1824
Mexico adopts a new constitution modeled on the Constitution of the United States, with one key difference: The Catholic Church is the country's only legal religion.

1829
Mexico abolishes slavery. Anglo-American Texians complain so strongly that an exception is made for Texas. Santa Anna becomes a national hero after helping to defeat Spanish forces attempting to retake Mexico.

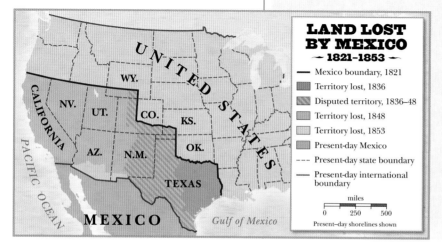

LAND LOST BY MEXICO
~ 1821-1853 ~

- ▬ Mexico boundary, 1821
- Territory lost, 1836
- Disputed territory, 1836–48
- Territory lost, 1848
- Territory lost, 1853
- Present-day Mexico
- --- Present-day state boundary
- ▬ Present-day international boundary

miles
0   250   500
Present–day shorelines shown

April 6, 1830
Mexico passes a law revoking all unfulfilled Texas empresario contracts, prohibiting new slaves, and closing the border to further immigration from the United States. Immigration from the U.S. increases in spite of the law.

1832
Law partners William B. Travis and Patrick Jack are arrested and imprisoned by the Mexican commander at Fort Anahuac. After a battle at Velasco, armed Texians force Mexican authorities to release them. The fort at Anahuac is abandoned.

1833
Santa Anna becomes President of Mexico as a Federalist. Texians draft a proposed constitution for a separate state of Texas within the Republic of Mexico. Stephen F. Austin takes the constitution and other requests to Mexico City.

1834
Stephen F. Austin is imprisoned in Mexico City. Colonel Juan Almonte tours Texas to investigate border security and the attitudes of Texians. Santa Anna becomes a Centralist and begins to consolidate power as a military dictator.

1835–36
Texas Revolution

June 29, 1835
William B. Travis leads an attack on Fort Anahuac. Captain Antonio Tenorio and his men surrender without a battle.

September 1, 1835
Stephen F. Austin returns to Texas.

September 20, 1835
General Cos lands at Copano on the Texas coast with 400 Mexican soldiers.

October 2, 1835
Texians drive off Mexican soldiers at Gonzales with the "Come and Take It" cannon.

October 9–10, 1835
Texians and Tejanos capture the presidio at Goliad.

October 28, 1835
James Bowie leads Texian forces to victory over Mexican soldiers at Mission Concepción.

November 3–4, 1835
Texians capture Fort Lipantitlán, near San Patricio, while most of the garrison is away and then fight off an attack by the main Mexican force, only to abandon the fort a few hours later.

November 7, 1835
Texians issue a Declaration of Causes, explaining why they are fighting against Santa Anna's government.

November 26, 1835
Forces under James Bowie skirmish with Mexican soldiers in the Grass Fight, just west of San Antonio.

December 5–9, 1835
Battle of Béxar is fought; General Cos raises a white flag on the 9th, signs the official surrender on the 11th, and leaves Texas.

February 23, 1836
Santa Anna and his army march into San Antonio. The siege of the Alamo begins.

The Alamo Siege and Battle

February 23, 1836
With the arrival of Santa Anna's troops in San Antonio, Texians and their Tejano allies withdraw to the Alamo. The siege begins.

February 24, 1836
James Bowie officially hands full command of the Alamo to William B. Travis. Travis writes his famous letter asking for reinforcements.

February 25–26, 1836
Mexican soldiers advance close to the Alamo, hiding in and behind a number of small houses called *jacales.* After a two-hour skirmish, the Alamo defenders drive the soldiers away. That night and the next a group of Alamo defenders sneak out and burn the jacales. Tejano Juan Seguín leaves the Alamo with a plea for help.

February 27, 1836
Santa Anna moves cannons closer to the Alamo and keeps up a steady bombardment.

March 1, 1836
Thirty-two men from Gonzales arrive to reinforce the Alamo.

March 3, 1836
James Bonham arrives at the Alamo with a message indicating (incorrectly) that Fannin is on his way with reinforcements. More than 800 Mexican reinforcements arrive in San Antonio, bringing the total to about 2,400.

March 4, 1836
Santa Anna holds a war council with his officers.

March 5, 1836
Santa Anna orders the Mexican Army to attack in the early morning of March 6.

March 6, 1836
The Mexican Army attacks at 5:30 a.m. All of the Alamo defenders are killed.

February 27, 1836
Mexican forces under General José Urrea attack 40 Texians under Colonel Frank Johnson in San Patricio; Johnson and others escape, but 28 Texians are killed or captured.

March 2, 1836
Convention at Washington-on-the-Brazos declares Texas independence from Mexico. Urrea's army wipes out a small group of Texians under James Grant at Agua Dulce. Grant is killed, ending efforts to take the Mexican city of Matamoros.

March 6, 1836
Fall of the Alamo (see column at left).

March 12–16, 1836
Men detached from Fannin's command lose a series of battles with Urrea's soldiers, thereby reducing Fannin's total force. Many of these men are captured and later executed, some with Fannin at Goliad and some separately.

March 19–20, 1836
After an all-day battle on the 19th, about 300 Texas soldiers under James Fannin surrender to General Urrea at Coleto Creek on the 20th.

March 27, 1836
James Fannin and 341 other men are executed at Goliad.

April 21, 1836
Texian troops under General Sam Houston defeat Santa Anna's army at San Jacinto.

May 14, 1836
General Santa Anna and interim Texas President David G. Burnet sign the two Treaties of Velasco, ending hostilities between Texas and Mexico. Both sides break the treaties almost immediately, and Mexico does not officially recognize Texas independence until the end of the Mexican War in 1848.

1842
Mexican forces invade Texas and briefly occupy San Antonio twice (in March and September). In retaliation, Texans raid Mexico, capture the towns of Laredo and Guerrero and fight a major battle near the town of Mier on December 25–26, where 179 Texans are captured.

1843
On their way to Mexico City, three prisoners captured at Mier escape. Santa Anna orders all 176 executed, but the governor of Coahuila refuses to do so. The Mexican government changes the sentence to death for every tenth man. On March 25 in the "Black Bean Episode," the men draw black and white beans from a jar. The 17 who draw black beans are executed.

December 29, 1845
U.S. President James Polk signs legislation making Texas the 28th state.

1846–48
The Mexican War, ignited by a dispute between the U.S. and Mexico over the boundary of Texas, leads to the U.S. winning much of what is now the American Southwest from Mexico (see map page 58). The Texas border is extended south to the Rio Grande.

1850
Texas gives up one-third of its claimed territory to the United States in return for a payment of $10 million, resulting in the modern boundaries of Texas.

1853
U.S. Minster to Mexico James Gadsden purchases 30 million acres in southern Arizona and New Mexico from Mexican President Santa Anna for $10 million (33 cents an acre). This completes the U.S. acquisition of what is now the American Southwest. The Mexican people are so angry at the cheap land deal that they later drive Santa Anna from office.

selected sources

Note: Abbreviations in parentheses are used in the Quote Sources below.

Almonte, Juan Nepomuceno. *Almonte's Texas*. Ed. by Jack Jackson. Trans. by John Wheat. Austin: Texas State Historical Association, 2003.

Barker, Eugene C. *The Life of Stephen F. Austin*. Nashville and Dallas: Cokesbury Press, 1925. Reprint. New York: Da Capo Press, 1968.

Davis, William C. *Three Roads to the Alamo*. New York: HarperCollins, 1998.

Callcott, Wilfrid Hardy. *Santa Anna*. Hamden, CT: Archon Books, 1964.

Castañeda, Carlos E., ed. and trans. *The Mexican Side of the Texan Revolution*. Dallas: P.L. Turner Company, 1928.

DeShields, James T. *Tall Men with Long Rifles*. San Antonio: Naylor Company, 1935.

Edmondson, J.R. *The Alamo Story*. Plano, TX: Republic of Texas Press, 2000.

Gaddy, Jerry J., comp. *Texas in Revolt*. Ft. Collins, CO: Old Army Press, 1973.

Hansen, Todd. *The Alamo Reader*. Mechanicsburg, PA: Stackpole Books, 2003. (AR)

Hardin, Stephen L. *Texian Iliad*. Austin: University of Texas Press, 1994.

Huffines, Alan C. *Blood of Noble Men*. Illustrated by Gary S. Zaboly. Austin: Eakin Press, 1999.

Jenkins, John H., ed. *The Papers of the Texas Revolution*. 10 vols. Austin: Presidial Press, 1973. (PTR)

James, Marquis. *The Raven*. Indianapolis: Bobbs-Merrill, 1929.

Johnson, Frank W., and Eugene C. Barker. *A History of Texas and Texans*. 5 vols. Chicago: American Historical Society, 1914.

Lindley, Thomas Ricks. *Alamo Traces*. Lanham, TX: Republic of Texas Press, 2003.

Matovina, Timothy M. *The Alamo Remembered*. Austin: University of Texas Press, 1995.

Santos, Richard G. *Santa Anna's Campaign Against Texas 1835–1836*. Waco, TX: Texian Press, 1968.

Seguín, Juan N. *A Revolution Remembered*. Edited by Jesús F. de la Teja. Austin: Texas State Historical Association, 2002.

Smithwick, Noah. *The Evolution of a State*. Compiled by Nanna Smithwick Donaldson. Austin: University of Texas Press, 1983.

Winders, Richard Bruce. *Sacrificed at the Alamo*. Abilene, TX: State House Press, 2004.

web sites

Handbook of Texas Online. http://www.tsha.utexas.edu/handbook/online/

Sons of Dewitt Colony Texas. http://www.tamu.edu/ccbn/dewitt/dewitt.htm

Southwestern Historical Quarterly. (SHQ) http://www.tsha.utexas.edu/publications/journals/shq/online/

Links to Some Texas History Primary Source Documents on the Internet. http://home.austin.rr.com/rgriffin/texhisdocs.html

quote sources

Numbers in bold refer to page(s) in this book where a quote is found, followed by the speaker, the source identified by author's last name or abbreviation as indicated in bibliography above, and the page(s) where quote can be found in the source. Some references are to multiple quotes from a single speaker.

11. Almonte: Almonte 253. **13.** Williamson: PTR v. 1, 195. **14.** Travis: Davis 453. Tenorio: SHQ v. 4 no. 2, 190–202. **14–15.** Harris: SHQ v. 4 no. 2, 85–127. **16.** Cos: PTR v. 1, 297; Austin: Barker 434; Santa Anna: Callcott 108–9. **17.** Travis: PTR v. 1, 385; Austin: PTR v. 1, 472. **20.** Mason: Johnson v. 1, 270. **21.** Moore: DeShields 17; Texian Interpreter: Gaddy 34. **22.** Smithwick: Smithwick 75, 71. **23.** Seguín: Seguín 76; McCulloch description: SHQ, v. 40, no. 1, 26–34. **24.** Bowie: Johnson v. 1, 279–80; Smithwick: Smithwick 80. **25–26.** Declaration: PTR v. 2, 346–48. **26.** Milam: Johnson v. 1, 352. **27.** Mexican officer (José Sánchez-Navarro): Hardin 90 & Edmondson 244. **28.** Autry: PTR v. 3, 105. **29.** Santa Anna: PTR v.3 114. **31.** Neill: PTR v. 3, 424; Smith: PTR v. 3, 458–9. **32.** Houston: PTR v. 4, 30; Neill: PTR v. 1, 14. **33.** Houston: PTR v. 4, 46; Jameson: PTR v. 4, 59; Neill: PTR v. 4, 127. **34.** Bowie: AR 19–20; Travis: AR 17; Crockett: AR 140. **35.** Menchaca: AR 505. **37.** Bowie: AR 19; Bowie/Travis: AR 24–25. **39.** Sutherland: AR 142–4. **40.** Seguín: AR 197; Esparza: AR 97; Travis: AR 32. **41.** Santa Anna's reply: AR 331–2. **42.** Travis: AR 32 & AR 34. **43.** Eyewitness (Robert M. Coleman): Lindley 15; Fannin: PTR v. 4, 398–9; Travis: AR 34 **44.** Fannin: PTR v. 4, 455. **44–45.** Travis: AR 37–8. **46.** Mexican officer (de la Peña): AR 424. **47.** Urissa: AR 485. **48–49.** Santa Anna's order: AR 338. **49.** Jameson: PTR v. 4, 303; Santa Anna: AR 341. **50.** Shouting soldiers: Hardin 139 & AR 486; Baugh: AR 73; Travis: AR 77; Esparza: AR 99; Mexican soldier: AR 486; De la Peña: AR 423–24. **51–52.** Almeron & Susanna Dickinson: AR 46. **52.** Becerra: AR 456–7. **53.** Almonte: AR 367. De la Peña: AR 427; another officer (José Sánchez-Navarro): AR 412. **54.** Santa Anna: AR 340–1; Urissa: AR 485. **54–55.** Ruiz: AR 501. **57.** Houston: PTR v. 6, 75.

selected postscripts

Juan Almonte accompanied Santa Anna to Washington, D.C., in 1836 and served as Mexican Minister to the United States from 1841–45 and 1853–56. He also served at various times as minister to Great Britain, France, and Spain and became involved in the French invasion of Mexico in 1862 and the establishment of Austrian Archduke Maximillian as Emperor of Mexico in 1864. Almonte died in Paris in 1869.

Stephen F. Austin returned from his mission to the United States in June 1836. That fall, he lost to Sam Houston in the first regular election for President of the Texas Republic but accepted the position of Secretary State.

He died on December 27, 1836, at the age of 43.

Susanna Dickinson, widowed with a baby and no money, married four more times. The first three were relatively brief: two ended in divorce—unusual at the time—and one ended when yet another husband died. Finally in 1857, she found a lasting, marriage to a successful man and lived a happier life, celebrated as the most famous survivor of the Alamo. She died in 1883.

Enrique Esparza and his mother and siblings stayed in San Antonio after the battle. Esparza later married and had seven children. He farmed for awhile in Atcasosa County, south of San Antonio, and

returned to his hometown as a farmer and wagon driver. He was discovered as an Alamo survivor in 1901, and gave several interviews about his experiences. Esparza died in 1917.

Sam Houston became the first regularly elected President of the Texas Republic in October 1836 and later served a second term. After annexation, Houston served as U.S. Senator and Governor of Texas. When Texas seceded from the Union on the eve of the Civil War, Houston refused to take the oath of loyalty to the Confederate States of America and was removed from office. He died in 1863.

James Neill was in Gonzales on the day the Alamo fell, spending $90 of his own money to buy medical supplies for the Alamo defenders. Commanding two cannons in Houston's army, he was seriously wounded in a skirmish the day before the Battle of San Jacinto. Neill led an expedition against the Indians in 1842 and was appointed an Indian agent two years later. He died in 1845.

Santa Anna was taken to Washington, D.C., after his surrender and returned to Mexico in 1837. He lost part of his leg fighting a French blockade in 1838 and regained his popularity. From 1839–55, Santa Anna served six different, often brief, terms as President and lost a series of

decisive battles as a general in the Mexican War. He spent several periods in exile and was finally allowed to return to Mexico in 1874. He died there two years later.

Juan Seguín led the only Tejano unit in the Battle of San Jacinto, was the only Tejano in the Senate of the Texas Republic, and served two terms as mayor of San Antonio. Due to conflicts with Anglo squatters on city land and suspicions of his connections with Mexico, he left office and spent six years in Mexico, where he fought against U.S. forces during the Mexican War. Seguín returned to Texas after the war, but later settled in the Mexican town of Nuevo Laredo, where he died in 1890.

index